The Truth
About The Sun

poems by

Jamie Cooper

Finishing Line Press
Georgetown, Kentucky

The Truth About The Sun

For Nicole

Copyright © 2022 by Jamie Cooper
ISBN 978-1-64662-807-0 First Edition
All rights reserved under International and Pan-American Copyright Conventions. No part of this book may be reproduced in any manner whatsoever without written permission from the publisher, except in the case of brief quotations embodied in critical articles and reviews.

ACKNOWLEDGMENTS

Some of the poems in this manuscript have appeared previously in the following publications:

"Polygraph"—*The Colorado Review*
"Handmade Boy"—*decomP*
"Earth Boy Leading Raincloud Horse"—*The Idle Class*
"The Truth About The Sun"—*TYPO*
"Notes on a Renaissance Essay"—*The Idle Class*
"Family of Flags"—*The Idle Class*
"Sermon"—*Parthenon West Review*
"Olympic Curse," "The Settlers," and "No Weather"—*Bitterzoet Magazine*

Publisher: Leah Huete de Maines
Editor: Christen Kincaid
Cover Art: Jamie Cooper
Author Photo: Jamie Cooper
Cover Design: Elizabeth Maines McCleavy

Order online: www.finishinglinepress.com
also available on amazon.com

Author inquiries and mail orders:
Finishing Line Press
PO Box 1626
Georgetown, Kentucky 40324
USA

Table of Contents

Polygraph 1

Handmade Boy 2

Earth Boy Leading Raincloud Horse 4

The Truth About the Sun 6

The Standard of Perfection 7

Enkidu's Dream 8

Nebuchadnezzar's Dream 9

Calpurnia's Dream 10

Electra's Dream 11

Notes on a Renaissance Essay 13

Family of Flags 14

Sermon 15

The Settlers 16

Olympic Curse 18

No Weather 19

Polygraph

As if to expose them
for the imposters that they are
we attached crude instruments
to their roots & stems
& scrutinized each response to stimuli
& whether we threatened to strike a match
& singe their leaves
or were just pretending
they could discern our intent
& if we sang or played sweet songs
they shared this pleasure eagerly
with the others
locked away in nearby rooms.

We'd learned to speak to them with tenderness
though they make no effort even to unfold
a solitary petal in reply.

But perhaps there are strange signals
smuggled aboard each oxidized vessel
voyaging invisibly to our bloodstream
so that if there were something
they wished for us to know
we would know it, suddenly,
& with a green clarity
quickened by the sun.

We believe in the sentient garden
& that the rate at which water rises
from the roots of the philodendron
up through the stem
to the tip of each perceptive leaf
is electric
though none of this would hold up
in a court of law.

Handmade Boy

I.
I am the handmade boy
descended from the tribe
of counterfeit children
carved from the elements,
a piece of timber whittled to a torso,
limbs devised from driftwood.
Tangled in another's will
I dance my clumsy dance
wide eyes painted on my animated face
unblinking, crimson mouth unmoving
when the man speaks through me.
I am the master's adolescent everlasting
the father's voice concealed
behind the curtains of a donkey-cart tableau
personified in song.

II.
Whereupon the master activates an arm
or articulates a leg
he summons the blessed virgin
to his ballet.
I go, and it is done; the bell invites me.
I go with a birdcage strapped upon my shoulders.
I go riding into the ambush
with the rearguard of Charlemagne.

In the eyes of actual children
I am the masked aboriginal.

In the midst of a confetti snowfall
the ultraviolet lights illuminate me.

I once glowed miraculously
as I danced upon the surface
of the flooded rice fields.

In the ancient times
they buried my ivory brethren
in the tombs of kings.

Earth Boy Leading Rain-Cloud Horse

The boy dropped nude into the canvas pasture
has been given a steadfast mare for escort
into the foreground of a developing storm.
Some shared feature in the anatomies
of equine & adolescent set the painter's hands to work
until he fashioned each face equal in demeanor
& the fluid outlines of each figure's form
conveyed youth's symmetry.

In the end the mare remained unbridled
& unmounted by the boy,
& only the artist in his omnipotence knows
for certain whether the boy's jaundiced skin
is equal to the unsown field beneath his feet
or if the tenor of the storm-cloud was made
equivalent to the mare's smooth hide.

How long had they remained suspended, headless
in his room before their countenances became
abruptly clearer by the silk sweep of his brush?
Was he painter in horse-suit, pretending to be wild,
unaccountable to the vulgar gods of his
unfinished fable,
the pre-teen's pastel texture,
the myth abandoned to these makeshift effigies
of youth, stripped bare for future witness,
the boy, bold beyond his years,
sky the color of an untamed horse?

Stubborn little god that he is,
the painter returns to the canvas
over which he has dominion,
with each brushstroke, painting himself
a little further back into his childhood,
serenity in his gaze,

that first word still wet upon his lips:
Piz! Piz!
The companion he leads into first light.

The Truth About the Sun

Secretly, the savage knew the truth about the Sun,
that it did not sink nightly into the consecrated sea,
that the face of a saint submerged couldn't bring the rain,
but he went on pouring pails of water over the dancing girls,
& showering the skeletons of the recently deceased,
& erecting imaginary rainbows over the skins of dead pythons.
Even Merlin among the Hawthorns slumbering knew
the Sun didn't need the bleeding hearts of man to give him strength,
that he had no use for the fresh horses tossed into the sea
to help pull his chariot gleaming across the heavens.
Still, the savage shot his flaming arrows into the eclipse to help reignite
the dying god. He could not imagine a world without spells
where blood was rain & a feather was a cloud & flaming branches
& hot stones could stop the rising floods, where the foreskins
of the village boys wrapped in feathers could make the rain return,
a world that when he required the assistance of the winds
he could simply loosen the length of rope tied in a witch's knot
& in the time of drought could sink the likeness of a saint
in a pond with a moon in the middle of it shining from below.

The Standard of Perfection

The first orchid comes with instructions
for the grower entrenched in the digital age
the novice with a curiosity for variety
(the Virgin & the Vampire)
everything the novice needs to know
about light, water, humidity
the pests, the viruses, the disease
the location of the rhizomes & ovaries
& the amateur will be able to identify
the familiar exotic lavender corsage
but must know that their root systems
are adapted to either the porous terrestrial soil
or an aerial existence on the skin of a tree
& must understand the critical role
of nighttime temperatures
the amount of warmth they are accustomed to
why altitude & other natural conditions
must be considered in the cultivation
how in the greenhouse of our modern homes
under the fluorescent lights
the blooms called "Happiness," "Canary"
"Orion" & "Fortune Smiles"
grow singly & erect or in clusters
from the axils of their pseudo-bulbs
how the Odontoglossums alone comprise
more than 300 species
& how when they are judged
they are judged against the hypothetical
standard of perfection

Enkidu's Dream

Brother, I have seen a dark place
filled with the ghosts of vanquished kings.
It is the House of Dust.
& I can feel my soul still clutched
by the talons of that terrible bird
that will soon carry me to its black corridors.
What to make of all these dreams?
I first appeared to your mother in a dream
a wild man, half-beast that would
reconcile your soul
& appeared to my own mother
in the place of dreams
before emerging from the dark earth
glistening with stardust & sacred waters
fully-formed.
What becomes of the woman who dreams
of a beast born from her own flesh?
I became a woman for the king:
Love domesticated my soul.
Dearest brother,
How far will you travel when your wild companion
is delivered over to the land of dreams,
when there is no longer any earth left
for you to wander?

Nebuchadnezzar's Dream

What a time you chose to be born
as if to illustrate the power of almighty God
or was it nothing more than sickness or psychosis
that made you crawl along the ground
like a rabid beast, your beard
sweeping up the earth below
…a triumph of your enemies?
In the first vision you saw
 the fall of all the future ages
the collapse of the massive idol
made of precious metals
—bronze belly & thighs
 silver chest & arms
iron legs & feet
partly made from clay—
empire upon empire
crushed under the colossal stone
a golden head atop the rubble
& in the next vision
stood astonished at the image
of a towering elm
& saw how easily it fell
& with what rage.
But it was the third vision
In which you watched your wife
—always longing for her homeland—
strolling once more
through the lush Persia of her youth
under the vaulted terraces
thriving with exotic plants
& imported wildlife
a wonder of the world all her own
& understood that
Heaven alone consumes all kingdoms.

Calphurnia's Dream

All night long
they washed their hands in the blood
from the stone that bleeds
the blood that cleanses the republic
all night long the lions prowled outside our gates
the rest came smiling to the fountain
of a hundred bleeding spouts
while the dead battalions fought midair
& rained down blood
on the ghosts of the proletariats
I watched as the images I feared manifested
& knew in my heart that on this day
you would not be crowned a king
You who I have loved so long
absent in my dream, & in your place a stone
so that absence is the stone that pours forth
your spirit always into my hands to cleanse me.

Electra's Dream

These are the libation bearers
Ill-fated Electra among them
Praying to her father's altar for return
The slave-girls mourning by the mounded grave
Sent by the mother to regain some relief from wrathful sleep
Yet the restless dead rage on inside her dreams.
Still, sweet sister, as she lifts her cup, knows not for what to pray
As you listen, hidden from her
And hear a slave-girl speak your name: "avenger."
In the dark courtyard
A lock of hair gleaming in her hand
Your hair
She summons the spring, the great ancestral dead
Summons you, Orestes, a dark comrade by your side
To unlock the secret chambers of your manhood.
And with bare feet she follows the footpaths that lead into the brush
To you, dear brother, reincarnate
Who'll answer grief for grief with shining sword.
God of guilt, strong god, patron and tormentor
Bringer of exile and plague
Hear the fateful siblings now, as they catch fire in their bloody strife
For the woman who bred the wolves' raw fury.
O peak of guilt!
Son and avenger, justice and curse
You lash the father's spirit back to life.
Now, on the witches' Sabbath
The Serpent returns
With a warlord's lust for glory
Bringing the third libation.

A swift stroke for Aegisthus, vengeance performed
But here, before the hearthstone, the childhood dream
The oaths we swore
The mothering voice who mourns

Young Orestes dead
Reborn into the lion at her gates
(and a second mother mourns
Who nursed the dearest plague)
Only the rough work of the world
Can humanize the gods.
Still, we'll seize the doctrine
for our shield.
Still, we'll strain
to praise them.

Notes on a Renaissance Essay

One must be a "lover of strange souls"
to imagine the young Italian
plucking some inexplicable tune
from the strings of his newly-constructed harp,
meaning woven from the looms
into the tapestries that afforded him
the luxury of buying birds
only to set them free
in a place identical
to where he imagined the first man & woman
situated on the virgin soil
in which they planted the seed
of discontent
always the presence of some maternity
the urge to illuminate the grotesque
the corpse, the embryo
all the small strange creatures
that "other" Medusa
seen for the first time
as a rotting head
the body unfit for worship
until now
the initial hesitation
now a feverish intensity
the orphan child evolving
into the alchemist of such
unimaginable scenes.

Family of Flags

The first flag of our family
Is a tricolor flag
& like most flags it is a flag
of independence
though it must abide by the laws & protocols
of its use
its coat of arms
an omen of victory
an Aztec emblem:
an eagle on a cactus
with a serpent in its beak
for every citizen & soldier to salute.
The subsequent European flags
are marked with X-shaped iconography
Saint Andrew's Cross
as he suffered an X-shaped crucifixion
a prominent white X
blazoned on an azure field
rather plain
& like most flags it is a funeral flag
like the Union Jack that flew
steadfast over so many thrones
whose colorless X intersects
the cross of St. David
a flag whose emblem occupies
the territory of so many other flags
& of the two domestic flags
another flag marked X
an emblazoned star for each confederate state
along the ecclesiastical lines
an oblong flag like all the others
& like most flags it is a battle flag
but not a flag of victory
rather a relic of some former sovereignty
& all of its fallen & defeated sons

Sermon

Behind his bifocals
My father dozes in a pew during a true story of God.
He dreams the fog lift off winter wheelbarrows,
Magic in the absence of the magician,
And the night he was stabbed anonymously
In a bar fight.
But the way story goes,
The only woman in a mining town
Dies during childbirth,
Leaving the miners to care for the child,
Which they do.
For its purpose, there's a lot left out,
But I can't help but think one of the miners
Is the real father, and knows it,
So that when he picks him up in private,
He holds him tighter than the others,
Until he almost can't breathe,
And prays hard for a different ending.

The Settlers

So much depends on the soles of my shoes
on these misshapen intervals,
the alternating days of training and of rest,
that I can no longer tell the difference between practice
and the real deal,
out there under the candied lights,
can no longer tell if I am as common as I often feel.
It is something of a solace then that I can go unregarded
on the streets of my homeland,
an ordinary citizen weaving through the throngs
of other ordinary citizens,
a minor aspect of the shifting mass,
'the crush of humanity' as it's sometimes called.
Like the planet Earth, I imagine I have the aura of opalescence,
and in this breeds the slow silk of Budapest.
So much for the forces that chastise us into an indistinguishable panoply.
If there is one thing we can surmise from the true green air and its
abundance
It is to call this condition critical,
to advance a theory about the theatricality of sickness
 the boiled whites, the feeding tubes, the blips
and bleeps of the heart machine,
its green neon mountains and crevasses.
Under awnings, under apses, under dark pavilions,
under ordinary eaves,
the monster was his sickness or vice versa,
it grew inside him like a vine,
wrapping itself around his bones
constricting
until it wrung the last drop of calcium light.
From the long inventory of his illness
a few standout stanzas:

the night he paused mid-dream to document the absence of his pain
like an empty socket, the negative space of a gaping wound
like a collapsed star
he mourned the lack of clean, Windexed surfaces,
mourned the ancient gleam of light on water.

Olympic Curse

I do not recall if ever there was a figure
lingering too long at the threshold of my Slavic homestead
or if at some fateful instant I crossed paths with the custodial engineer
wielding a mop bucket, emptied of the requisite rakes and brooms
I recall pausing to sit quietly for a moment
in anticipation of every journey
but never with my feet propped up on my provincial table
I do not recall the gift of knives, the gift of clocks
or the gift of scarves on Russian holidays
have always welcomed the arrivals of pigeons and arachnids.
I remained hidden from friends and relatives for 40 days after I was born.
I've drunk every ounce of alcohol in my house
clutching the chilled glass with my palm until the last drop.
I drank the last glassful for luck
and always raised a lucky toast to my comrades
I've eaten chunks of food off the end of a knife
I've listened to the lucky ringing in my ears
felt the lucky itch of my eye sockets.
I often consider the living waters of the feminine Earth
its fertile future
and the purifying fires that burn with the spirits of our ancestors,
and filled with dread I often think about these evil winds
I've burned the effigy of my lesser self,
bathed in streams beneath new moons and thunder.

No Weather

It was no longer cold. Nor had it ceased or started to rain again. There were no clouds or sun, no stars or any moon. There was no migration of birds to warmer climates. No mammals retreating into hibernation in their many caves. The wind was not cold. There was no chill in the air coming off the water from the lakes or rivers. There was no storm approaching from the sea. It had not begun to snow. The lake was not alive under a layer of ice for the fisherman and his lures. There was no noonday sun. No mirage on the horizon in any desert. The cars were not covered in overnight frost. There was no warm current for the salmon swimming upstream. No pockets of warm air for the planes to navigate unsteadily. Indian summer had not arrived. It was not unseasonably warm. The clean white snow in the streets had not turned brown from exhaust. The water was not the perfect temperature, or any temperature at all. There were no warnings. No one was monitoring a tropical depression forming off the coast. No one had given it a woman's name. There was no snow above 10,000 feet. No frozen rain to fold the pines in half on your front lawn. The sky was not blue or clear or cloudless or heavy with a coming rain. You could not see your breath in the air. Nor would the blond hairs on your arms stand on end from the cold.

There was no need for layers, no need to peel the layers off one by one. No need for gloves or scarves or late summer sweaters. The desert had not grown cold at night. There was no need to build a fire. No need to light the furnace. No need to retrieve your grandmother's quilt from the wooden chest your father carved his name into. The power had not gone out. The hurricane lamps did not light up one by one in the windows of the houses in your neighborhood. Your mother had not slipped and fallen on the ice on the sanctuary steps on Christmas Eve while carrying a small child. There were no footprints in the snow the next morning leading to the backdoor of your house. You had not slept with the windows open listening to the rain. You had not dreamed again of a funnel cloud forming on the horizon. It was not May. It was not September. It was not any time of year outside that you could tell.

Inside, it can be any time of year. Inside, you are the god of weather. Wave your hand. You are the commander of many storms. Inside, you drag the demon out into the light.

Jamie Cooper is a poet and writer living in Portland, OR. He earned an MFA from the Iowa Writers' Workshop and is a recipient of a 2020 Oregon Literary Fellowship. His work has most recently been featured in *Blue Earth Review, Molotov Cocktail, Tempered Runes Press, Fractured Lit,* and elsewhere. He occasionally writes about the NBA for *UPROXX Sports*.

www.ingramcontent.com/pod-product-compliance
Lightning Source LLC
LaVergne TN
LVHW041526070426
835507LV00013B/1839